THE LITTLE RED BOOK OF KLOPP

First published 2019 by Macmillan
an imprint of Pan Macmillan
The Smithson, 6 Briset Street, London, EC1M 5NR
Associated companies throughout the world
www.panmacmillan.com

ISBN 978-1-5290-1207-1

1 3 5 7 9 8 6 4 2

A CIP catalogue record for this book is available from the British Library.

Illustrations by Isobel Mehta

Designed by Ambar Galan
Printed and bound by TJ International Ltd, Padstow, Cornwall

Visit **www.panmacmillan.com** to read more about all our books
and to buy them. You will also find features, author interviews and
news of any author events, and you can sign up for e-newsletters
so that you're always first to hear about our new releases.

THE LITTLE RED BOOK OF KLOPP

Gilezinho

MACMILLAN

CONTENTS

1 | On Klopp

'When I was a player, I played in empty stadiums. The fans, they were not banned – they were only not interested in the football we played.'

'I never succeeded in bringing to the field
what was going on in my brain. I had the
talent for the fifth division, and the mind for
the Bundesliga. The result was a career in the
second division. I realized my own limits before
others did. I quickly accepted it. To be upset
would have been a waste of time.'

'Does anyone in this room think that I can do wonders? I'm a normal guy from the Black Forest. My mother is very proud. I am the Normal One.'

'If it stinks of sweat in here, that's me. The game was so thrilling. I've seen wins that haven't felt this good.'

'I'm not too smart, but not silly. Not too funny, but not too serious. I'm a nice guy, I would say. Most of the time.'

'I was a very average player. I don't compare myself with these genius managers from the past. I couldn't believe that I was a professional footballer. I would have paid for being allowed to play football at that time.'

'I had a great childhood. It was totally idyllic. There were only five or six boys in that little village and we were the football team, the tennis team and the ski team. It was wonderful.'

'When I left school, the head said: "I hope you can do something in football because, if not, I have not the best feeling for your future."'

'If somebody beamed me into the year 2005, I would have been shocked. I would have been able to run naked through the streets of Mainz then. Nobody would have known my name.'

'With all these pictures on Twitter, it always looks like I am in restaurants and bars! I am not that type of guy.'

'The problem with my life is that I've said too much s**t in the past and no one forgets it.'

'Yes, it's true. I underwent a hair transplant. I think the results are really cool, don't you?'

'It was the fortune of my life to do exactly what my father had wanted to do. Any other job would have caused friction. My father wouldn't have understood if I wanted to become a florist. He wouldn't have said: "No problem, I'll buy the first bouquet." He would have thought I was crazy.'

2 | On Liverpool

'Liverpool was always a name.
The size of the club is always defined
by the things they have won, or the fan
base they have, or stuff like that. It is all
together. When I got the call I knew my
break was finished. It was only a feeling.
And that feeling, obviously, was right.'

'I'm not a dreamer. I am a football romantic. I love the stories and Anfield is one of the best places in the football world. Now I'm here. I'm a lucky guy. It's the biggest honour to be at one of the biggest clubs in this world. I'm looking forward to the intensity of football and how the people live football in Liverpool. It's a special club. I had two special clubs with Mainz and Dortmund and this role is the perfect next step for me to try to help.'

'Twenty-five years ago is a long time and a lot of people have tried to take the next title but history is like your backpack. We must not carry twenty kilos of history on our backs. This is a team of great potential. We must change performances because no one is satisfied. And **stop thinking about money – only football.**'

'My first meeting with the whole team I made downstairs in the dressing room and I brought in all the people working here at Melwood, because I didn't know them – obviously – but I was pretty sure a lot of the players don't know them as well. So I let them walk through the press room: "Do you know the name of all these people? They all work for you, all day, twenty-four hours, are there for you whatever you do, however the last result was. It's important you have a relationship."'

'When I sit here in four years I would say we won one title. If not, next time I will manage in Switzerland.'

'The history of this club shows you it is possible to win things. It's not that you need to be the most special manager in the world. This club gives you the power, the players, the teams that you can win, from time to time, big things.'

'We feel as a family, if I'm honest. I feel that we are here as a family. So we all work together, we all try to win together. Everybody is doing his piece – that's how it is. They are all on fire, all the time. They have all the Liverpool heart. We come in, go out, but they stay. They keep the standard.'

'I've met some Evertonians in the street and they've been friendly. I've had taxi drivers who have been Everton fans. They've been really nice. At the beginning I thought: "OK, maybe they're happy I'm here because they think that means Liverpool won't have any success for the next twenty years!"'

'1984? I was seventeen.
I probably had something else to do.'

On Liverpool's European pedigree

'I have no time, and I am not in the
mood for reflection, to be honest. It's a
year, I'm a year older and all this s**t,
but everything else is good. Not perfect,
but in a good way.'

On his first anniversary with Liverpool

'If I had said on my first day: "This is my club,"
then I would be lying. Today it is 100 per cent
true, and that is a big development. I feel
100 per cent responsible for pretty much
everything here, and that's how it is.'

'If I have to describe this club then it's a big heart and last night it was obviously like crazy, pounding like crazy. You could hear it and probably feel it all over the world. When I saw the boys after the game and saw the tears in their eyes, that's football and they are professionals and it's still like this. This club touches you like crazy, and it's like you feel much more than others in these moments.'

On beating Barcelona 4–0 to reach the Champions League 2019 Final

3 | On Language

'"Boss tha" is not a problem for me.
But I need more time to get better at Scouse!'

'I can speak like a waterfall.
But only in my own language.'

'Oh my God. It looks like the name of a snake. OK: "Gorra cob on." So if I'm not happy, I say: "Gorra cob on."'

'You don't understand? You should learn. There are some really good German explanations for some problems. But I don't know how to say it in English.'

'That's a very erotic voice by the way. The translator. Congratulations. Wow. Again please. Ha ha ha ha ha! Whoops-a-la!'

4 | On Managing

'One of the most important skills in this job is dealing with the pressure. I know myself since fifty years and I put, really, a lot of pressure on my shoulders, and I learnt to deal with that. I ignore the public pressure. Look, if you walk through a city and you think: "What is he thinking about me? What is he thinking about me?" You don't know these people but you're thinking about what they're thinking about. Most of the people I don't know. I'm not interested in their opinion. I'm responsible for my family, 100 per cent, and then my club.'

'I am not an idiot. I have the first and last words. It's enough. The middle – well, I am not a genius. We have a discussion. It's really easy to handle this.'

'One big head needed to roll – my one.'

On leaving Borussia Dortmund

'I'm a bit proud of my first red card as a coach. I approached the fourth official and said: "How many mistakes are allowed here? If it's fifteen, you have one more."'

'In these moments the boys need a push from outside. The fuel is really low – it's close to the end – and you need a little help from outside and an angry manager who gives you a little advice: "Run . . . or I kill you."'

'If, as a manager, I would overestimate any kind of performance, then I would be constantly up and down: "Oh my God, how good is he? He is so bad! F***ing hell, what is he doing here?"'

'I cannot make people happy. I never could. The ideal size of the squad is eleven and no one injured. Then they are all happy – a little bit exhausted but all happy. If you have twelve then you already have one who thinks: "Why am I out?" Everything will be fine. But if someone has a problem with it, he will have a problem with me.'

'I'm responsible for our bad performances; the players are responsible for our good performances. That's quite an easy deal.'

'Arsène likes having the ball, playing football, passes. It's like an orchestra. But it's a silent song. I like heavy metal.'

'It's a big honour to talk to Sir Alex. For a manager it's nearly the best thing you can do, to sit there and listen. I needed ten minutes to understand what he was saying and then it was OK. Maybe he is the greatest ever, the John Lennon of football or something like this.'

'I respect Arsène and Sir Alex, a lot, for what they did for football and stuff, but the game changed a lot. I think the first fifteen years round about from these two guys, they were like a holiday in comparison to what they had in the last fifteen years of their job. I'm fifty and I feel young for all things of life. But I'm too old for this.'

'It'll be fun, especially because I meet my landlord, I think for the first time since he left Liverpool and I came here. We have a lot of things to talk about. The plumbing issue, electricity, the pool and stuff like that. So, Brendan, hope you are in good shape and we can sort a few things.'

'I don't ask for an easy way. But it's not like the good old times when you had your squad for six weeks in pre-season and spent one week **team-building by going to a forest in Sweden with nothing to eat**, like I did when I was young. That's not possible anymore.'

'If you break rules, you have to be fined for it. No problem with that. It's completely normal. If there was no rule against it we, as managers, would constantly celebrate on the pitch and you would say: "That's nice!" I don't think anybody thought it's massively wrong. It's a fine, I pay it. We make mistakes, but usually I learn from it. At least over a long period.'

'Eighteen years to do 600 games. Mmm. So another eighteen years would mean . . . sixty-nine. Yeah . . . so . . . furthermore. Hopefully I'm healthy then still. And then we count what happened.'

On reaching the milestone of 600 games as a manager

5 | On Music

'The best band in the world? My mother said it, my father said it. Number one – The Beatles.'

'Let's talk about six, baby!
Let's talk about you and me'

On winning Liverpool's sixth Champions League trophy

'I couldn't have been a rock star. Although I do sing "Country Road" very loudly on the PlayStation karaoke game.'

6 | On the Beautiful Game

'The experience is more important than the result. That's our code. We are the vanguard of the regular guys in the pub. They want us to run and fight. You can only get in touch with the game's emotions via pace and action. Football is theatre. If we don't put on a superb performance, only two guys will be sitting there at the end.'

'Whoever stays the course, never gives up, never stops working, will be rewarded at the end. That's my fundamental belief. We will keep on fighting until someone tells us: "You can stop now. The season's over."'

'This club and this city have to learn to take moments like that for what they are. In life, you cannot ignore the negative things that have happened. If you can change them, change them. If you can't change them, ignore them. If you get up in the morning and the first hour is bad, does that mean you go back to bed? No.'

'Football's just a game. If you don't enjoy the game, then don't play it! The results are very, very important, actually the most important – because it means it keeps the business going, that's how it is, that's our life – but the ninety minutes, it's a game.'

'I love this game because you can win against better teams. If you work better together than the other team, that's what I really like. That's why I love to be a manager. I love this game.'

'I wasn't even sure the ball from Dejan was in for a long time. But it was and, well . . . good! I've had a lot of games in my life and not too many like this. If you read it in a book you think, "Oh, nice!", but it is really rare.'

On the 4–3 comeback against Borussia Dortmund to go through to the Europa League semi-final

'I show my team very often Barcelona but not the way they play. Just the way they celebrate goals. Goal number 5,768 in the last few weeks and they go "Yeessss!" like they never scored a goal. This is what I love about football. That's what you have to feel all the time. Until you die. And then everything is OK.'

'I relish the total intensification, when bangs go off everywhere, when it feels as if people don't dare to breathe.'

'I'm either all in or not at all. It's like a marriage – there are good times and bad times. Why should the sun be shining out of my ass the whole time?'

'Whose idea was this to have two games in the semi-final? Strange!'

'They did not show this game on TV? They show every f***ing game in Germany!'

On the 3–0 win at Derby in the League Cup

'To be honest I was not interested in the history before the game because maybe a few tried already to do the seventh time, or whatever. Now, I like it. To be honest, I like it! So that's cool.'

After seven straight wins at the start of the 2018/19 season

'We all have a few weaknesses but that's not a problem. We're not in the world to be perfect. We have to try to get better every day – that's important. Make the world a little bit nicer, more beautiful, things like this. But nobody has to be perfect.'

'It was not that we are so much better, but it was so different, so brave. It was big-balls football. But we are Liverpool. We are different. We have been different the whole campaign and we want to be different again. We have a chance. That is all.'

'If people cannot enjoy our football then I can't help them. There were games last season when we were flying and the opponents collapsed, like Watford, then we had the big games like Roma and Manchester City. I get constantly confronted with the question – something is missing. Of course it could be better, but in the end, in the games we won we were always the better side. That's pretty rare. Not one lucky game.'

'I know it will be the headline but the number of interruptions in the game was not cool. We won the Fair Play Award two times in England and tonight we looked like butchers with the number of yellow cards. It was clever of PSG, especially Neymar, but a lot of other players went down like there was something serious. We were not that calm any more, rather frustrated, and negative frustration does not help. That is a job for us to deal with.'

7 | On Losing

'When I gave the first interview, I was very disappointed. After the second one ten minutes later, I was feeling better. In thirty minutes, I'll probably feel like we won the match.'

'We feel down but now we have to stand up. Only silly idiots stay on the floor and wait for the next defeat.'

'We have to believe in the long-term project. Nobody wants to hear it but losing is part of football. I love driving to training in the morning and working with the boys, even if it's difficult. You can't give up because you're losing. You have to try again in the next game.'

'That's one of the worst things I ever heard in life. Win the game, have respect for the player of the other team. I thought: "Really, what did he say?" If they thought before the game that Loris Karius is a weakness, then I don't know which game they were looking at. Maybe they watched games from Mainz. I am really looking forward to playing Bournemouth again because of this.'

On Bournemouth defender Steve Cook describing goalkeeper Loris Karius as a 'weakness'

'We made our goal, but because we weren't good enough today the linesman thought: "Well, you don't make world-class goals if you play this s**t."'

'I would really like to change my personality, but I can't forget this f***ing loss against Crystal Palace . . . After the goal on eighty-two minutes, I saw many people leaving the stadium. I felt pretty alone at that moment.'

'I have no clue how it will feel when I go to the next final. I lost the last five and then you think: "Ooh, really?" It's better that you lose the semi-final than the final, as nobody talks about who lost the semi-final.'

On losing the 2016 League Cup final to Manchester City

'We can change nothing now, but we can change something tomorrow morning. Tonight, we feel rubbish. OK, we feel s**t.'

'It's weird, because after you lose a game, everything always feels completely different. People even feel the weather is worse than it is.'

'I am not fine. I'm the opposite of fine. I have lost games in my life before, so I know how to deal with that, but you can't avoid the feeling the night after the game. We all feel really, really bad, and the trip home will not be the best trip we've ever had in our lives. We wanted everything, and got minus something.'

On the 2018 Champions League final

'It was a big moment in the game. I know if you say something like that after you've lost, you sound like a bad loser. But for me that was kind of a harsh challenge because the arm is there and it was like wrestling. It was very bad for Mo, very bad for us, very bad for Egypt. That's part of the sport I don't like, but things like this can happen. I don't know what would have happened had Mo played on. We will never know that.'

'People will say I am weak or a whiner. I am not. I accept it. It's not like I wake up in the morning and think: "Ramos."'

'We played good football, but we lost 3–1, so I don't think in ten years people will talk about that. The other decisive moments were the goals.
They were quite strange . . .'

'I do not have the personality to wait for problems but I know they will come. Nothing is ever perfect. We will have problems. We had it today and we had it over the years. So let's play.
Let's play football.'

8 | On Players

'I told my players during the break: "Since we're here anyway, we might actually play a bit of football."'

'If that's not a bulls**t story, I'll eat a broomstick!'

About the rumour Mats Hummels was moving to Manchester United

'We have signed a fantastic player, but someone who is an equally fantastic person I think. He has a lovely family also – adding a person like this to our dressing room only makes us even stronger. He has the ability and mentality to play at the highest level in a number of positions. He can play 6, 8 and 2. This is cool.'

On Fabinho

'These young players are our future. If we handle them like horses, then we get horses. We don't have to sprinkle magical dust on them: "And now you can play football . . ." They know how to play.'

'I read and hear about him being a wonderful role model for Egypt, North Africa, for the wider Arabic world and for Muslims. This of course is true – but he is a role model full stop. Regardless of race or religion, country or region of birth. The only labels we should put on Mo is what a good person he is and what a fantastic footballer he is – and by the way, the first part of that is more important in life than the second.'

'We played against him when he was at Basel and we didn't know him. We played with Dortmund against him and it was: "What the f***!"'

On first encountering Mo Salah

'If I spoke to a player now and he told me: "If you were playing in the Champions League next year then I would be really interested," I would put the phone down. That is what I would say to players. It is about pushing the train, not jumping on a running train.'

'I want to get the feeling that you can only imagine playing for one club. If you don't have that feeling, if you think you have to talk to others, leave it. If you haven't caught fire after I told you about the club, you shouldn't come here.'

'Crazy players love me
– I don't know why.'

'I came from a very small club where I played for eleven years and then was the manager. Everyone treated me like a friend. Then I went to Dortmund and after the pre-season we were friends. The players were young, even younger than my sons, so I was for them a pretty old friend.'

'I want people around me to do well. That's what life is about. I don't have to step on people's toes. I don't have to threaten punishment to get them to perform. I have to show players targets in a way that they automatically want to achieve them.'

'We will wait for him like a good wife
waiting for her husband who is in jail.'

On Mats Hummels

'In the morning he looks horrible.
We have no choice than to drink enough
until he looks better in our eyes.'

On Roman Weidenfeller

'Shinji Kagawa is one of the best players in the world and he now plays twenty minutes at Manchester United – on the left wing. My heart breaks. Really, I have tears in my eyes. Central midfield is Shinji's best role. He's an offensive midfielder with one of the best noses for goal I ever saw.'

'The most important thing is for the players to be prepared to be a little wild. You can run and then you can miss. No problem. Don't worry. Come back again. We can do better and will do better. It's OK.'

'Each striker could write a book
about these moments when you score
without knowing how it actually works,
how you did it. You need each ball in
the perfect way, but it's so rare that
it happens like that.'

'Coutinho can play. Don't believe everything in the press or that there are offers here and there and that the minute after the offer has been entered, it should already be over. We are not like George Orwell where everybody knows everything immediately. We have exactly the situation we wanted and no other.'

On the rumours Coutinho could be leaving Liverpool

'I don't like that actually – this little chip when he came out of the goal. That's not too cool for a manager. If it works, then it's cool. I've never had a Brazilian goalkeeper. Maybe you buy that as well.'

'It doesn't make it any easier to run your heart out when you've just woken up in a five-star hotel. Too much comfort makes you comfortable.'

9 | On Money

'Money isn't the most important thing. It is important, of course. I am not Mahatma Gandhi.'

'That's the problem these days.
Whatever bulls**t you say, nobody will
forget it. On the other side, it is still kind
of true. I couldn't imagine the world
would change like that from two and
a half years ago. One hundred million
was a crazy amount of money. Since
then the world has changed completely
and we have signed the most expensive
goalkeeper and all that stuff. We don't
care what the world around us is
thinking, like Man United didn't
care about what I said.'

10 | On Critics

'The pundits, former players most of them, forgot completely how it felt when they got criticized. Especially the Neville brothers; the one who was the manager, he obviously should know that too much criticism never helps. He showed he struggled with the job to judge players so why do we let him talk about players on television?'

'How should that work? What do we do? We don't play Champions League or what? Gary should come over and tell me how that would work. I don't want to be too critical but sitting in an office and talking about football is completely different to doing the job.'

'I think my smartest decision in life was not to use social media. I don't read it if people criticize me on social media. They can write whatever they want and it would never faze me because I don't know it. I don't read it.'

'I'm not interested in criticism,
I'm more interested in the thoughts
of the people.'

11 | On Life

'I believe that everything in life happens for a good reason. One day we'll find out why . . .'

'We have to start new, use the experience but not rely on it. The best way is when you are experienced and you use your new knowledge and start again like a virgin.'

'Most things in life I learned because somebody gave me the right advice in the right moment, without me asking. I was a lucky guy. I met some nice people in the beginning – teachers, coaches. And of course my parents and all that stuff. I think that's what life should be. You make your own experiences and whether they're good or bad you share them so somebody else can avoid the same mistakes.'

12 | On Winning

'The best word I can say to describe this is: "Boom!"'

On beating Manchester City 3–0

'You have to get information in each situation. You'll never find me three days after a win, drunk in a hedge and still celebrating.'

'The only alternative is to carry on. We have to do this, not become more passive and become a counter-attacking team. We could not come here and be like that.'

'We are really desperate to win something, and the best would be the league, but we don't know when that will happen. So we should have the best time of our lives until that happens.'

'Did you ever see a team like this, fighting with no fuel in the tank? I am so happy for the boys, all these people and my family. They suffer for me, they deserve it more than anybody. It was an intense season with the most beautiful finish I ever could have imagined. We'll celebrate together, we'll have a sensational night.'

On winning the Champions League with Liverpool

'I get all these messages saying:
"Wow, unbelievable, blah blah blah," and
I don't even feel it. If you are in the job,
you know there are still twenty games to play.
I've been a sportsman since I was five years old,
running races, athletics. If you think after 300
metres, "I have him," then you will never win.'

'How do you explain to a blind person
what a colour is?'

*On being asked by a Schalke fan what the secret
is to winning the Bundesliga*

13 | On Fans

'It's crazy what happened in this stadium. It's phenomenal. People here are as happy as if they had a second hole in their backside.'

'If the audience wants emotions, but you offer lawn chess, either you or they must look for a new stadium. It's always about making the crowd happy. It's about producing games with a recognizable style. When matches are boring, they lose their rationale.'

'During the week at our training sessions, there were a lot more people. "If you don't win it now, I'll support Schalke." That's what someone said. Three thousand people got an autograph. He didn't. Even though he was wearing a yellow shirt. You mustn't forget there might be children around.'

14 | On German Football

'It would have been crazy if we won the Champions League last season. I think we would have lost our minds. I would have loved to watch that story if it was a movie. A story like the Cleveland Indians in *Major League*. But it really would have been very crazy. So that is why everything is OK.'

'If we should finish second this summer,
I'll find a truck and drive it through
my garden. If nobody will rejoice,
I'll do it alone.'

'You win and you lose, but you're with
people you like. You're at home. You
belong. That's what we all want. Ten
million people want to belong here.'

'When BVB last won here, most of my players were still being breastfed. We have a bow and arrow and if we aim well, we can hit the target. The problem is that Bayern has a bazooka. But then Robin Hood was quite successful.'

'Mkhitaryan fits us like an arse on a bucket. What he offers is exactly what we need.'

'My glasses are in the Borussia Dortmund museum. When we beat Bayern, Nuri Şahin did it. I don't know what it looked like at the end – I lost my glasses! I have a second pair of glasses but it is hard to find them without my glasses.'

'My motivation is for people to tell and retell. That's what this club is about. Its most important pillar is the stories it has written since its foundation. That's why I love experiencing this time here so much. It gives us the chance to write such stories.'

'Bayern go about football in the same way that the Chinese go about industry. They look at what the others are doing, and then they copy it with other people and more money. And then they overtake you.'

'If I were him, I'd thank God that someone had the idea of hiring me every time I walked into the Bayern training ground. I don't know if Bayern would have got one fewer point without Sammer.'

On Matthias Sammer, former Borussia Dortmund icon turned Bayern Munich Sporting Director

'Götze has gone because he is Guardiola's personal chosen signing and he wants to play with Guardiola, in his style. It's my fault. I can't make myself fifteen centimetres shorter or start speaking Spanish.'

'To bring the team to the Champions League final is the biggest moment in my career? No, that was 2004, getting promoted with Mainz. If you had known the money we had, the circumstances we had, nobody needed us in the first league. If I win the Champions League, though, I will have to think about this question again.'

'The best news today is that football is over for 2014. Any criticism that we receive now is justified. We are standing here like complete idiots and it's completely our own fault.'

'The only thing I can say is that it was great. London's the town of the Olympic Games. The weather was good, everything's OK, only the result is so s**t.'

On losing the Champions League 2013 final to Bayern Munich

'If anyone tells me: "What a shame!" tonight, I'll punch the glass out of their hands without so much as a word. Please enjoy the evening and don't worry – we will definitely be back.'

On losing the German Cup final to Bayern Munich in 2014

15 | On Staying Out of the Public Eye

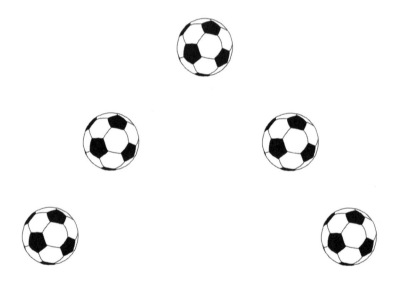

'In extreme situations, you have to think fast. At one of my mates' stag parties, we all dressed up as Father Christmas – fully masked.'

16 | On Tactics

'Tactical behaviour is not like riding a bike. You have to practise all the time.'

'I'm not looking for a fight, so I will answer even the stupid questions. If you say we've been found out, what does that say about the work of opposition coaches for the last few years? Were they unable to see what our game is?'

'People were asking: "It's good you don't concede, but where is the free-flowing football?" I sit here and think it's like a kid getting a nice present for Christmas and then asking: "Where is the other one?"'

'*Gegenpressing* is the world's best playmaker.'

'We had a good plan in the first half but conceded two goals, so you can throw your plan in the purple bin.'

'I am not the guy who is going to go out and shout "we are going to conquer the world" or something like this. But we will conquer the ball. Yeah. Each f***ing time!'

'I am not a dreamer. I don't dream that we can be there or there. Other people can do that but we have to build a ground for these dreams. We need to play football and that is 80 per cent of the season, if not 90 per cent, the hardest work. The 10 per cent is the day when you go "bang, bang, bang" and win 5–0. Wow. That is football.'

'When everything is brilliant and we score goals, you always ask about defending and how we can fix that. We fixed that – kind of – and it always happens that the first step is it costs you a bit of fluency and creativity. That is a completely normal thing. When we fix that, I can't say in the first moment to the boys: "But that's not enough offensively." That would be crazy! Bringing in one player would change everything? That is bulls**t and you know it.'

'We don't run more than others, but we run without taking breaks. We train all week to be sharp for ninety minutes. And we have a well-defined system. We don't sting everything in sight like a swarm of hornets. We lure the opponent and then sting him.'

'I could play them all together. We could play 4–1–4! Hang on, I've forgotten a player, haven't I? OK, 4–1–5!'

On fielding all his attacking players

17 | On England

'I like what we in Germany call *Englischer Fußball* – rainy day, heavy pitch, everybody is dirty in the face and they go home and can't play for the next four weeks.'

'I read in Germany that there are still transfers in the Bundesliga for £5 million. You can imagine that happening in England? No chance! Yet it is similar quality.'

'I made a party in my house, and invited all the people here, and I said: "We start at seven." At seven, only the Germans were in, and I'm thinking: "Hey, where are they?" And then they all came, half-pissed already, and it's like, we don't do that! We drink where we go. "Where have you been?" And it's this bar, and this bar . . .'

'I am really impressed that we are at a Champions League press conference talking about things like this. I really don't understand the business anymore. I love Harry, too. Actually, that's not important for Russia. It's just an English thing. Pochettino loves Kane – and who do I love? That's the question. It's a waste of time.'

18 | On His Face

'My face would have warranted a five-match ban. I don't recognize myself sometimes on the touchline.'

'Surprised? No. What can I say? They gave me three games for my face in Naples.'

'If someone is silly enough to want to see my face for ninety minutes during a game, I cannot change the world.'

'I look very tense. I killed my teeth over twenty years, rrr rrr rrr, looking like this. It's not that I wanted to do it. I think the public knows my ugly face because I have this constantly.'

19 | On His Wife

'She wrote a book for children. It's like Harry Potter, but on football. There's no Harry Potter flying on his f***ing broomstick – just football.'

'I just got told, apparently I'm leaving the club because my wife kicked me out and that I'm having an affair with a player's wife. Wow. I mean – lovely players' wives, of course, but . . .
I have rarely been confronted by rumours that interest me, but I think we can bury that one straight away. I love my Ulla as much as ever, with all my heart. She hasn't kicked me out; she's probably had a thousand reasons, not because of any other woman but because I'm a little bit stupid.'

20 | On Opinions

'It's only an opinion in that moment. Did I change my opinion? Yes. That's true. But it's better to change your opinion than never have one. Whatever people say and bring it up again and again, I have had worse days in my life and worse things happen to me. We have the players we wanted. I am fine with that.'

'It's not important what people think of you when you arrive. It's important what they think of you when you leave.'

Acknowledgements

Thanks must first go to all the journalists who have had the pleasure to bring Jürgen Klopp's words into the public domain. Kloppisms could stretch to several volumes, but for a definitive biography of the man, Raphael Honigstein's *Klopp: Bring the Noise* is heartily recommended.

Along with Isobel Mehta's wonderful illustrations, Jonathan Harris, Robin Harvie and Matt Cole helped bring this book into the world, and special thanks too to Helena Gonda.

Thanks to my wife Eliane for giving me my Brazilian name Gilezinho, and for bearing with me as I embarked on a new life of writer, editor and garden centre employee. Literature and horticulture – a great team.

Finally thanks, of course, to Herr Klopp himself. The world is a brighter place with him in it.